own your voice™

by
Deanna Geneva Lorianni & Meghan Codd Walker
Co-Founders, Zuula

This journal does not replace professional therapy.
Please seek the guidance of a licensed professional
for supporting your mental wellness.

Copyright © 2022 Zuula Consulting, LLC

All rights reserved. You cannot use or reproduce any part of this book for any manner without the copyright owner's prior written permission. To request permission, please contact the publisher at:
OwnYourVoice@zuulaconsulting.com.

ISBN: 978-1-7350394-0-4

Cover Design & Layout By: Helm & Hue
Printed by: IngramSpark

Zuulaconsulting.com

Dedicated to ...

All the women in our lives who lift up and inspire us.

The women working hard to break down stereotypes and inequalities around the world.

You, for being the unique and wonderful woman that you are.

Introduction

Own Your Voice™ is about you, for you.

This book is a freewriting journal designed to help you better understand why and how your voice matters. The goal is to find inspiration, look within yourself, and emerge as a confident communicator!

Why did we create this book?

As women, society tells us how we're allowed to share our voice. And too often, expectations and cultural norms box us in.

We speak up — and we're *forceful*.
We get angry — and we're a *bitch*.
We explain something — and we're *interrupted*.
We get emotional — and we're *weak*.

All of these judgments start defining our self-worth, our identity, and our voice from a young age. And we take these feelings and experiences with us through adulthood — unless we actively work to leave them behind. In fact, women are more likely to underestimate their abilities than men — and will discount positive feedback about what they can do well.* These judgments can keep us from participating equally in society and creating action, for ourselves and others.

Whether you lack confidence, are unsure how to share your opinion, or face another roadblock, you can remove the wall — and embrace your power. You can own your voice!

*Gerdeman, Dina. "*How Gender Stereotypes Kill a Woman's Self Confidence.*" Harvard Business School Working Knowledge. 2019. https://hbswk.hbs.edu/item/how-gender-stereotypes-less-than-br-greater-than-kill-a-woman-s-less-than-br-greater-than-self-confidence. Accessed 11 August. 2020.

About This Journal

With the Own Your Voice freewriting journal, our goal is to inspire you to tap into your hidden thoughts and feelings. Although we do not intend the book to replace professional therapy, we hope you gain tools to help you uncover the voice within you. After seeing women flourish from a single freewriting workshop, we want to make this growth possible for more women. Together, we can push society forward by finding strength in being and voicing our true selves.

To achieve this goal, each weekly writing prompt shares the following traits:

An inspiring quote by a successful, strong woman

A freewriting prompt that relates to her quote

A place for you to freewrite on that week's topic

Each prompt builds on the other to help you open, uncover, and explore all the facets that make you, you.

Freewriting Entries

We created each prompt specifically as a freewriting exercise. Freewriting is a writing strategy designed to elicit thoughts and feelings that you otherwise ignore or shut down.

With each prompt, you'll do the following:
1. Set a timer for 10 minutes.
2. Write the first thoughts that come to your mind without stopping until the 10 minutes finish.
3. Stop writing the moment the 10 minutes ends.
4. Reflect on what you wrote.

When we say don't stop, you truly will not stop writing during these 10 minutes. Even if you feel stuck and don't know what to say, you'll write thoughts like this: *I'm stuck. I don't know what to write. My brain feels like mush, mush, oatmeal, like oatmeal. My mom used to make oatmeal for me and always call me Honey when she served it...*

See how that went? Random thoughts that connect until details emerge?

As soon as the timer starts, you begin writing any and all thoughts that the prompt provokes. And you never stop to worry whether:

- A thought was good or bad
- The thoughts connect
- Grammar was correct
- A sentence was a complete thought
- Or any other type of judgment

In fact, don't focus on the quality of your writing at all! With these prompts, we're focusing solely on awakening the emotions that you're hiding within you. And, if you arrive at a quote or a prompt that you feel doesn't speak to you: Do the prompt anyways! Truly. Do every single prompt in this book without judging it beforehand.

If you give in to this emotion telling you, "Nah, skip this one," then you're doing exactly what this book is helping you undo: You're judging something before exploring its worth. The goal here is to remove the voice that judges your thoughts and feelings — so you can arrive at new perspectives and open insights.

When you first try a freewrite, the process may feel awkward if you've never done it before. And that's totally okay. The more you do it, the more comfortable you'll feel being vulnerable in your thoughts. On the flip side, freewriting may feel liberating to you as you finally give yourself space to feel, think, and write without judgment. During our Own Your Voice workshops, we've seen women have both responses — and everywhere in between.

So, if you feel stuck during a prompt, keep going. Just write the thoughts you're having! The goal is to keep your hand moving and writing whatever comes to the top of your mind for the entire 10 minutes. We promise that once you get going on a prompt, a whole world of insights and feelings will emerge on the page. And those 10 minutes will go by more quickly than you expected!

Why does freewriting work?

One of the biggest ways we can hit writer's block — and emotional blocks — is because we automatically start judging our ideas as soon as they exist. Rather than give these feelings space for reflection, we edit away in our mind what we instantly deem as wrong or invalid or stupid or any other negative trait we can tell ourselves. Once we enter this cycle, we now spend our energy critiquing our thoughts — instead of allowing them to emerge and offer insights on who we are and how to grow. We also often miss out on the deeper perspectives hiding within, because we're so focused on familiar, surface concerns.

> **Remember:** No one needs to see what you wrote for your prompt. And no bad or good thought exists. Your thoughts are for you. So who cares how you wrote something? By removing the negative voice — that judgment filter — you open up opportunities for your emotions to emerge. From here, your ideas can exist. And once they do, your voice can thrive.

This journal is but a step in your journey.

We hope that what you awaken and reflect on enables you to deepen your relationship with yourself. By doing so, we hope you'll uncover details about who you are that you otherwise would've chosen to judge and ignore. With this awareness, you can move beyond how society defines you — and allow your own identity and how you feel to be the only definition you know. So you can feel confident in being yourself.

And, you can finally **own your voice**.

Cheers and with love,
Deanna & Meghan

> "When no one speaks and the whole world is silent, then even one voice becomes powerful."

– Malala Yousafzai

About Malala

Girls' and women's education activist, human rights activist, youngest Nobel Prize laureate
born 1997

What does your voice mean to you?

....
....
....
....
....
....
....
....
....
....
....
....
....

Own Your Voice

Week 1

> Without courage we cannot practice any other virtue with consistency. We can't be kind, true, merciful, generous, or honest.
>
> – Maya Angelou

About Maya

Writer, poet, civil rights activist, one of the first African American women to have a screenplay produced as a film, received the Presidential Medal of Freedom
1928 – 2014

What's something right now you that need to feel courageous about, and why?

....
....
....
....
....
....
....
....
....
....
....

Own Your Voice

Week 2

> "What you do makes a difference, and you have to decide what kind of difference you want to make."
>
> – Jane Goodall

About Jane

Primatologist, anthropologist, considered world's top expert on chimpanzees, UN Messenger of Peace born 1934

What difference do you make?

Own Your Voice

Week 3

> **Independence is happiness.**
> – Susan B. Anthony

About Susan
Social reformer, women's rights activist, suffragist
1820 – 1906

How do you embrace your independence?

Own Your Voice

Week 4

> "There will be people who say to you, 'You are out of your lane.' They are burdened by only having the capacity to see what has always been instead of what can be. But don't you let that burden you."
>
> – Kamala Harris

About Kamala

First woman-, first Asian American-, and first African American elected to serve as U.S. Vice President; highest ranking woman elected to serve the U.S. federal government
born 1964

What external limits do you want to break free from?

....
....
....
....
....
....
....
....
....
....

Own Your Voice

Week 5

> **The world will see you the way you see you, and treat you the way you treat yourself.**
>
> – *Beyoncé*

About Beyoncé

Singer, songwriter, actress, one of the best-selling musicians in history, second-most-honored woman by the Grammys born 1981

Do you like the way you treat yourself? Why or why not?

....
....
....
....
....
....
....
....
....
....
....
....

Own Your Voice

Week 6

> Understand that failing is a process in life, that only in trying can you enrich yourself and have the possibility of moving forward.
>
> – Sonia Sotomayor

About Sonia

First Hispanic and Latina Justice in U.S. Supreme Court
born 1954

How has something you failed in helped you grow?

....
....
....
....
....
....
....
....
....
....
....
....
....

Own Your Voice

Week 7

> "Don't look at your feet to see if you're doing it right; just dance."
>
> – Anne Lamott

About Anne
Writer, political activist, 2010 California Hall of Fame inductee
born 1954

Describe something you've been overanalyzing recently.

....
....
....
....
....
....
....
....
....
....
....
....

Own Your Voice

Week 8

❝ I know that all I can do is be the best me that I can. And live life with some gusto.

– Michelle Obama

About Michelle

First African American first lady of the United States, author
born 1964

How can you live your life with gusto?

....
....
....
....
....
....
....
....
....
....
....
....

Own Your Voice

Week 9

> We have been marginalized for a long time, and now is the time for women to stand up and become active without needing to ask for permission or acceptance.
>
> – Tawakkol Karman

About Tawakkol

Co-recipient of 2011 Nobel Peace Prize, and first Yemeni, first Arab woman, and first Muslim woman to win a Nobel Prize
born 1979

Where in your life do you ask for permission to be you, and why?

....

....

....

....

....

....

....

....

....

....

....

Own Your Voice

Week10

> This is the only way I have of doing things, and the only way I have of living.

– Arundhati Roy

About Arundhati

Author, human rights- and environmental activist, recipient of the Man Booker Prize and Sydney Peace Prize
born 1959

How can you embrace your own unique way of living?

....
....
....
....
....
....
....
....
....
....
....
....

Own Your Voice

Week 11

> "I am able to get up and dust myself off and keep moving. I'm very stubborn."
>
> – Rita Moreno

About Rita

Actor; first Puerto Rican and only Latinx to win Emmy, Grammy, Oscar, and Tony awards
born 1931

How can being stubborn help you?

....
....
....
....
....
....
....
....
....
....
....
....
....

Own Your Voice

Week 12

> Each and every one of us has the capacity to be an oppressor. I want to encourage each and every one of us to interrogate how we might be an oppressor and how we might be able to become liberators for ourselves and for each other.
>
> – Laverne Cox

About Laverne

Actor, LGBTQ+ activist, first openly transgender nominee for a Primetime Emmy Award in any acting category
born 1972

How are you pushing down who you are?

....
....
....
....
....
....
....
....
....
....

Own Your Voice

Week 13

> It is invaluable to have a friend who shares your interests and helps you stay motivated.

– Maryam Mirzakhani

About Maryam
Mathematician, first woman and first Iranian to receive the Fields Medal
1977 – 2017

Describe a woman in your life who motivates you, and why.

....
....
....
....
....
....
....
....
....
....
....
....
....

Own Your Voice

Week 14

> **Embrace the glorious mess that you are.**
>
> – Elizabeth Gilbert

About Elizabeth
Author
born 1969

What feels messy right now that you embrace?

Own Your Voice

Week 15

> I do not wish [women] to have power over men but over themselves.

– Mary Wollstonecraft

About Mary
Writer, philosopher, women's rights advocate
1759 – 1797

What makes you feel powerful?

Own Your Voice

Week 16

> "You can never leave footprints that last if you are always walking on tiptoe.

– Leymah Gbowee

About Leymah

Liberian peace activist, led Women of Liberia Mass Action for Peace that helped to end the Second Liberian Civil War
born 1972

What are you tiptoeing around right now?

Own Your Voice

Week 17

> **If you haven't forgiven yourself something, how can you forgive others?**
>
> – Delores Huerta

About Delores
Labor leader and activist, co-founder National Farmworkers Association, recipient of Presidential Medal of Freedom and Eleanor Roosevelt Award for Human Rights
born 1930

What's something you want to forgive yourself for but haven't yet?

....
....
....
....
....
....
....
....
....
....
....
....

Own Your Voice

Week 18

> Power is not brute force and money; power is in your spirit. Power is in your soul. It is what your ancestors, your old people gave you. Power is in the earth; it is in your relationship to the earth.
>
> – Winona LaDuke

About Winona

Native American activist, environmentalist, economist
born 1959

What is something powerful that you inherited from the women in your life?

Own Your Voice

Week 19

> Be less curious about people and more curious about ideas.

– *Marie Curie*

About Marie

First woman to win a Nobel Prize, first person to win Nobel Price twice, first person to win Nobel Prize in two different scientific fields (physics & chemistry)
1867 – 1934

Describe a new idea you've had recently.

Own Your Voice

Week 20

> **To fly we have to have resistance.**
>
> – *Maya Lin*

About Maya

U.S. architect, designer, sculptor; Creator of the Vietnam War Memorial; Recipient of the National Medal of Arts and Presidential Medal of Freedom
born 1959

How is something in your life creating friction while also building strength?

....
....
....
....
....
....
....
....
....
....

Own Your Voice

Week 21

> **Where there is a woman, there is magic.**
>
> – Ntozake Shange

About Ntozake
Playwright, poet
1948 – 2018

What makes you magical?

....
....
....
....
....
....
....
....
....
....
....
....
....
....
....
....

Own Your Voice

Week 22

> "I am a woman with thoughts and questions and shit to say. I say if I'm beautiful. I say if I'm strong. You will not determine my story — I will."
>
> — Amy Schumer

About Amy
Comedian, actor
born 1981

In what ways are you allowing someone else to tell your story?

....
....
....
....
....
....
....
....
....
....

Own Your Voice

Week 23

> "Hate is too great a burden to bear. It injures the hater more than it injures the hated."

– Coretta Scott King

About Coretta
Author, civil rights activist
1927 – 2006

What hate are you holding that you'd rather release?

....
....
....
....
....
....
....
....
....
....
....
....

Own Your Voice

Week 24

> When I dare to be powerful, to use my strength in the service of my vision, then it becomes less and less important whether I'm afraid.

– Audre Lorde

About Audre
Writer, civil rights activist
1934 – 1992

How are you strong?

Own Your Voice

Week 25

> **Do what you feel in your heart to be right, for you'll be criticized anyway.**
>
> *– Eleanor Roosevelt*

About Eleanor
Former First Lady of the United States, activist
1884 – 1962

When has following your heart led you to a good decision?

....

....

....

....

....

....

....

....

....

....

....

....

....

Own Your Voice

Week 26

> **One must be frank to be relevant.**
>
> – *Corazon Aquino*

About Corazon

First woman to be president of the Philippines, first democratically elected president in Asia
1933 – 2009

In what ways do you feel relevant?

....
....
....
....
....
....
....
....
....
....
....
....

Own Your Voice

Week 27

> Instead of looking at the past, I put myself ahead twenty years and try to look at what I need to do now in order to get there then.
>
> – Diana Ross

About Diana

Singer; record producer; recipient of the Presidential Medal of Freedom; only woman with #1 singles as a solo artist, as part of a duet, as part of a trio, and as an ensemble member born 1944

Who do you want to be in 20 years?

Own Your Voice

Week 28

> Being in the depths of sadness is just as important an experience as being exuberantly happy.

— *Marlene Dietrich*

About Marlene

Actor, singer, humanitarian, considered the 9th greatest female screen legend of classic Hollywood cinema by the American Film Institute
1901 – 1992

What is something you feel sad about and haven't shared with anyone?

Own Your Voice

Week 29

> **If they don't give you a seat at the table, bring a folding chair.**
>
> – Shirley Chisholm

About Shirley

First African American to run for the Democratic U.S. presidential nomination, first African American senator, co-founder Congressional Black Caucus
1924 – 2005

Where in your life do you feel you need to bring your own chair, and why?

....

....

....

....

....

....

....

....

....

....

Own Your Voice

Week 30

> Some people are old at 18 and some are young at 90. Time is a concept that humans created.

– Yoko Ono

About Yoko
Musician, artist, peace activist
born 1933

How old do you feel, and why?

....
....
....
....
....
....
....
....
....
....
....
....
....
....

Own Your Voice

Week 31

> "The most common way people give up their power is by thinking they don't have any."

– Alice Walker

About Alice
Novelist, short story writer, poet, political activist
born 1944

How can you own your power?

....
....
....
....
....
....
....
....
....
....
....
....
....
....

Own Your Voice

Week 32

> **Run to the fire; don't hide from it.**
>
> – Meg Whitman

About Meg
Business executive, philanthropist, political activist
born 1956

What fire in a relationship have you been avoiding?

Own Your Voice

Week 33

> At the end of the day, we can endure much more than we think we can.
>
> – Frida Kahlo

About Frida
Painter
1907 – 1954

What are ways that your strength has surprised you?

....
....
....
....
....
....
....
....
....
....
....
....
....
....

Own Your Voice

Week 34

> **None of us can know what we are capable of until we are tested.**
>
> – Elizabeth Blackwell

About Elizabeth

Physician, first woman to receive medical degree in the U.S.
1821 – 1910

What has tested your strength recently?

....
....
....
....
....
....
....
....
....
....
....
....
....
....

Own Your Voice

Week 35

> So often in life, things that you regard as an impediment turn out to be great, good fortune.

– Ruth Bader Ginsburg

About Ruth

Associate Justice of the United States Supreme Court
1933 – 2020

Describe something that once felt challenging and ended up giving you new opportunities?

....
....
....
....
....
....
....
....
....
....
....
....
....
....

Own Your Voice

Week 36

> Don't let anyone rob you of your imagination, your creativity, or your curiosity.
>
> – Mae Jemison

About Mae

Astronaut, first African American woman to travel to outer space, physician, engineer, professor
born 1956

Pick one: imagination, creativity, or curiosity. Why is this trait important to you?

....
....
....
....
....
....
....
....
....
....
....
....
....
....

Own Your Voice

Week 37

> The most effective way to do it, is to do it.

– Amelia Earhart

About Amelia

Aviation pioneer; author; first woman to fly solo, nonstop across the U.S. and across the Atlantic Ocean
1897 – 1939

How does waiting affect a decision you need to make?

....
....
....
....
....
....
....
....
....
....
....
....
....

Own Your Voice

Week 38

> "Life need not be easy, provided only that it is not empty."
>
> – Lise Meitner

About Lise
Physicist, co-discoverer of nuclear fission
1878 – 1968

How have challenging times positively impacted who you are today?

....
....
....
....
....
....
....
....
....
....
....
....
....
....

Own Your Voice

Week 39

> "I really think a champion is defined not by their wins but by how they can recover when they fall."
>
> – Serena Williams

About Serena

Tennis player, won the most Grand Slam single titles of any athlete in Open Era born 1981

How are you your own champion?

....
....
....
....
....
....
....
....
....
....
....
....
....

Own Your Voice

Week 40

> "Never retract, never explain, never apologize. Just get things done, and let them howl."
>
> – Nellie McClung

About Nellie
Author, social activist, suffragist
1873 – 1951

How does apologizing hold you back?

Own Your Voice

Week 41

> "Cows run away from the storm while the buffalo charges toward it — and gets through it quicker. Whenever I'm confronted with a tough challenge, I do not prolong the torment; I become the buffalo."
>
> – Wilma Mankiller

About Wilma

First woman to serve as principal chief of the Cherokee Nation, native- and women's rights activist
1945 – 2010

How can you charge toward a storm in your life right now?

....

....

....

....

....

....

....

....

....

Own Your Voice

Week 42

> Do not live someone else's life and someone else's idea of what womanhood is. Womanhood is you.

– Viola Davis

About Viola

First African American woman to achieve the Triple Crown of Acting, only woman of color to win a Primetime Emmy Award for Outstanding Lead Actress in a Drama Series
born 1965

What does being a woman mean to you?

....
....
....
....
....
....
....
....
....
....
....

Own Your Voice

Week 43

> One of the criticisms I've faced over the years is that I'm not aggressive enough or assertive enough, or maybe somehow, because I'm empathetic, I'm weak. I totally rebel against that — I refuse to believe that you cannot be both compassionate and strong.

– Jacinda Ardern

About Jacinda

New Zealand Prime Minister, youngest leader to represent the Labor Party, the world's youngest woman to serve as head of government when elected, the 2nd woman in the world to give birth while an elected head of government born 1980

What stereotypes do you rebel against that make you strong?

....
....
....
....
....
....
....
....

Own Your Voice

Week 44

> "A woman with a voice is by definition a strong woman."
>
> – Melinda Gates

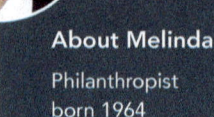

About Melinda
Philanthropist
born 1964

What does having a voice mean to you?

....
....
....
....
....
....
....
....
....
....
....
....
....
....
....
....
....

Own Your Voice

Week 45

> **Listening is the tool required for life.**
>
> – Joy Harjo

About Joy

First Native American U.S. Poet Laureate, musician, playwright
born 1951

How does listening strengthen your voice?

....
....
....
....
....
....
....
....
....
....
....
....
....
....

Own Your Voice

Week 46

> "You must never so much think as whether you like it or not, whether it is bearable or not; you must never think of anything except the need and how to meet it."
>
> – Clara Barton

About Clara

Nurse, suffragist, civil rights activist, humanitarian, founder of the American Red Cross
1821 – 1912

Describe something in your life that you want to achieve no matter how difficult it is.

Own Your Voice

Week 47

> I encourage women to step up. Don't wait for somebody to ask you.

– Reese Witherspoon

About Reese

Actor, producer, entrepreneur, children's and women's rights advocate
born 1976

Describe one way right now that you can step up.

....
....
....
....
....
....
....
....
....
....
....
....

Own Your Voice

Week 48

> I've never had a humble opinion. If you've got an opinion, why be humble about it?

– Joan Baez

About Joan
Singer/songwriter, musician, social activist
born 1941

How can being humble hold you back?

Own Your Voice

Week 49

> **To find your own truth, I think, is one of the most powerful practices.**
>
> *– Alicia Keys*

About Alicia

Musician, singer, songwriter, actress, philanthropist
born 1981

What does living your own truth mean to you?

....
....
....
....
....
....
....
....
....
....
....
....
....
....

Own Your Voice

Week 50

> "Follow your passion. Whatever you're doing, do your best at all times and make it as correct as possible.

– *Katherine Johnson*

About Katherine

Recipient of U.S. Presidential Medal of Freedom, first woman to co-author a NASA research paper, helped NASA send the first astronaut to the moon
1918 – 2020

How does something you're passionate about define who you are?

Week 51

> **Bitches get stuff done.**
>
> – Tina Fey

About Tina
Actor, writer, producer, playwright
born 1970

How can being assertive help you?

....
....
....
....
....
....
....
....
....
....
....
....
....
....
....
....

Own Your Voice

Week 52

You did it!

You freewrote for 52 weeks and opened up thoughts and feelings that perhaps you haven't explored recently — or ever.

We hope that this process encouraged you to look within and find inspiration for all the ways that you are you. And how expressing your thoughts and feelings can inspire you to own your voice and be your true self, rather than hold back.

From here, we encourage you to keep exploring your feelings. Use a journal to think through what emerged on these pages. And, perhaps even try these prompts again! As you've self-reflected and grown in these past 52 weeks, so has your voice. By redoing these prompts, you may find that you have new perspectives now. Imagine what you can uncover by continuing your growth!

We also encourage you to explore: How you can you help other women own their voices, too? That person could be your mother, your daughter, your sister, or even your neighbor. Perhaps, the insights you've gained within these pages can inspire others! Share a copy of this book with them. And, maybe even use these prompts as conversation starters to help those you love explore their thoughts and feelings with you.

When women come together, we grow together. With that unity, we can make our voices heard! As Malala Yousafzai reminds us, we only need one voice to make a difference in the world. And this change starts with you.

We wish you the best as you continue your journey in understanding your voice and owning your strength.

Thank you for bringing us with you!
Deanna & Meghan

Quote Attributions

Pg. 7: "Malala Yousafzai Speaks at Harvard." *YouTube*. Uploaded by Harvard Foundation. 17 Oct. 2013, https://www.youtube.com/watch?v=e1tOe4SKbLU. Accessed 10 Feb. 2021.

Pg. 9: Angelo, Maya. *USA Today*. 5 March 1988. Compiled by *WikiQuote*. (n.d.), https://en.wikiquote.org/wiki/Maya_Angelou. Accessed 10 Feb 2021.

Pg. 11: Goodall, Jane. "An Evening With Jane Goodall." *The Jane Goodall Institute New Zealand*. (n.d.): http://www.janegoodall.org.nz/dr-jane-tours-of-new-zealand/tomorrow-beyond/im:2409/. Accessed 10 Feb. 2021.

Pg. 13: Susan B. Anthony, "365 Great Quotes for 2017 (Inspiring Words for the New Year)." *Inc.* (n.d.), https://www.inc.com/bill-murphy-jr/365-great-quotes-for-2017-inspiring-incredible-and-interesting-words-for-the-new.html. Accessed 10 Feb. 2021.

Pg. 15: Harris, Kamala. *Black Girls Lead 2020 conference*. Wright, Jasmine. "Harris talks ambition in women of color after personal attacks during Biden's VP search," *CNN*, (n.d.), https://www.cnn.com/2020/07/31/politics/kamala-harris-ambition-remarks/index.html. Accessed 10 Feb. 2021.

Pg. 17: Beyoncé. "Exclusive: Beyoncé Wants to Change the Conversation." Interview by Tamar Gottesman. *Elle*, 4 April 2016, https://www.elle.com/fashion/a35286/beyonce-elle-cover-photos/. Accessed 10 Feb. 2021.

Pg. 19: Sotomayor, Sonia. "Sonia Speaks: An Interview With Justice Sonia Sotomayor." Interview by Kevin Urich. *The Progressive*, 9 Feb. 2013, https://progressive.org/dispatches/sonia-speaks-interview-justice-sonia-sotomayor/. Accessed 10 Feb. 2021.

Pg. 21: Lamott, Anne. *Bird by Bird: Some Instructions on Writing and Life*. Anchor Books. 1994.

Pg. 23: Obama, Michelle. "Oprah Talks to Michelle Obama." Intervew by Oprah. *O, The Oprah Magazine*, April 2009, https://www.oprah.com/omagazine/michelle-obamas-oprah-interview-o-magazine-cover-with-obama/all. Accessed 10 Feb. 2021.

Pg. 25: "Renowned activist and press freedom advocate Tawakul Karman to the Yemen Times: 'A day will come when all human rights violators pay for what they did to Yemen.'" *Yemen Times*, 17 June 2010. Archived from the original, *WayBackMachine*, 1 Jan. 2012. https://web.archive.org/web/20120101154044/http://www.yementimes.com/defaultdet.aspx?SUB_ID=34255. Accessed 10 Feb. 2021."

Pg. 27: Roy, Arundhati. "Arundhati Roy: Why Happiness Is a Radical Act." Interviewed by Charlotte Sinclair. *Vogue*, 27 July 2017, https://www.vogue.co.uk/article/arundhati-roy-interview. Accessed 10 Feb. 2021.

Pg. 29: Moreno, Rita. "Rita Morena Reflects on Anita, Awards, and Accents." Interviewed by NPR Staff. *Weekend Edition Sunday*, NPR, 7 March 2013, https://www.npr.org/2013/03/10/173726066/rita-moreno-reflects-on-anita-awards-and-accents. Accessed 10 Feb. 2021.

Pg. 31: "Laverne Cox receives the Stephen F. Kolzak Award at GLAAD Awards." *YouTube*, uploaded by GLAAD, 13 Apr. 2014, https://www.youtube.com/watch?v=mRkLhB34Xb0. Accessed 10 Feb. 2021.

Pg. 33: Mirzakhani, Maryam. "Being Effective and More: Interview With Maryam Mirzakhani as Research Fellow." Interviewed by Efat Jalalvanad. *LinkedIn*, 15 Aug. 2014, https://www.linkedin.com/pulse/20140815064935-110297096-being-effective-and-more/. Accessed 10 Feb. 2021.

Pg. 35: Galla, Brittany. "In Honor of Elizabeth Gilbert's 50th Birthday, Here Are 50 of Our All-Time Favorite Quotes by the Author." *Parade*. 18 July 2019, https://parade.com/902715/brittany_galla/in-honor-of-elizabeth-gilberts-50th-birthday-here-are-50-of-our-all-time-favorite-quotes-by-the-author/. Accessed 10 Feb. 2021.

Pg. 37: Wollstonecraft, Mary. *A vindication of the rights of woman: with strictures on political and moral subjects*. 1792. Boston: Peter Edes for Thomas And Andrews. Early English Books Online Text Creation Partnership, 2011, https://quod.lib.umich.edu/e/evans/N19251.0001.001/1:7?rgn=div1;view=fulltext. Accessed 10 Feb. 2021.

Pg. 39: "Speech by Minister of State Michelle Müntefering honouring Leymah Gbowee at the presentation of the Bonn International Democracy Prize." (2018, 21 Nov.). *German Information Centre Africa*. https://germanyinafrica.diplo.de/zadz-en/-/2162860. Accessed 10 Feb. 2021.

Pg. 41: "Forgiveness and Letting Go Quotations." *University at Buffalo School of Social Work*, (n.d.), https://socialwork.buffalo.edu/resources/self-care-starter-kit/additional-self-care-resources/inspirational-materials/forgiveness-and-letting-go-quotations.html. Accessed 10 Feb. 2021.

Pg. 43: "New Year, New You: Start 2015 Native Style." *PowWows.com*. 14 Jan. 2015, https://www.powwows.com/new-yearnew-youstart-2015-native-style/. Accessed Feb. 10, 2021.

Pg. 45: Curie, Marie. *Living Adventures in Science*. Quoted by Henry Thomas and Dana Lee Thomas, 1972. Archived by WikiQuote, (n.d.), https://en.wikiquote.org/wiki/Marie_Curie. Accessed 10 Feb. 2021.

Pg. 47: "Maya Lin Artist Overview and Analysis." *TheArtStory.org*, 2021. Content compiled and written by Laura Fiesel. Edited and revised, with Summary and Accomplishments added by Ruth Epstein. First published on 28 Mar 2016, https://www.theartstory.org/artist/lin-maya/. Accessed 10 Feb 2021.

Pg. 49: Shange, Ntozake. *Sassafrass, Cypres & Indigo*. St. Martin's Press, 1982.

Pg. 51: Vineyard, Jennifer. "Read Amy's Powerful Speech About Confidence." *Vulture*, 2014, Compiled from "Gloria Awards and Gala," 1 May 2014, https://www.vulture.com/2014/05/read-amy-schumers-ms-gala-speech.html. Accessed 10 Feb. 2021.

Pg. 53: "Coretta Scott King Quotations. Quotations From the Civil Rights Leader and Activist." *ThoughtCo.*, 23 Feb. 2018, https://www.thoughtco.com/coretta-scott-king-quotes-3530856. Accessed 10 Feb. 2021.

Pg. 55: Lorde, Audre. *The Cancer Journals*. 1980. Wikiquote, https://en.wikiquote.org/wiki/Audre_Lorde. Accessed 10 Feb. 2021.

Pg. 57: Roosevelt, Eleanor. *How to Stop Worrying and Start Living*. 1948. Wikiquote, (n.d.), https://en.wikiquote.org/wiki/Eleanor_Roosevelt. Accessed 10 Feb. 2021.
Pg. 59: "Corazon Aquino Quotes. Philippine President, Lived 1933 – 2009." *ThoughtCo.*, 25 March 2017, https://www.thoughtco.com/corazon-aquino-quotes-3530055. Accessed 10 Feb. 2021.
Pg. 61: "50 Inspirational Quotes to Help You Achieve Your Goals." *Entrepreneur*, 2 Feb. 2017, https://www.entrepreneur.com/article/287870. Accessed 10 Feb. 2021.
Pg. 63: Dietrich, Marlene. "How to Be Loved." *Ladies' Home Journal*. 1954. Compiled by *Quotations By Women*, (n.d.), https://quotationsbywomen.com/authorq/26059/. Accessed 10 Feb. 2021.
Pg. 65: Chisolm, Shirley. "A Seat at the Table: Digital Exhibit." *Edward M. Kennedy Institute*, 2019, https://www.emkinstitute.org/explore-the-institute/exhibits/a-seat-at-the-table. Accessed 10 Feb. 2021.
Pg. 67: "10 Common Problems Old Souls Experience at Least Once in Their Life." *Thought Catalog*, 28 Sept. 2015, https://thoughtcatalog.com/koty-neelis/2015/09/10-common-problems-old-souls-experience-at-least-once-in-their-life/. Accessed 10 Feb. 2021.
Pg. 69: "Alice Walker." *Encyclopedia Britannica online*. Encyclopedia Britannica, Inc., (n.d.), https://www.britannica.com/explore/100women/profiles/alice-walker. Accessed 10 Feb. 2021.
Pg. 71: Whitman, Meg. "Taking On A Turnaround." *LinkedIn*, 25 Feb. 2013, https://www.linkedin.com/pulse/20130225195955-71744402-taking-on-a-turnaround/. Accessed 10 Feb. 2021.
Pg. 73: "Frida Kahlo Quotes." *ThoughtCo.*, 10 Feb. 2019, https://www.thoughtco.com/frida-kahlo-quotes-3525389. Accessed 10 Feb. 2021.
Pg. 75: "10 Quotes From Pioneering Women to Guide You in Business and Life." *Inc.*, (n.d.), https://www.inc.com/amy-vetter/10-quotes-from-pioneering-women-to-guide-you-in-business-life.html. Accessed 11 Feb. 2021.
Pg. 77: "Ruth Bader Ginsburg: Rejected by the Firm." *YouTube*. Uploaded by MAKERS, 12 June 2012, https://www.youtube.com/watch?v=IdFUmU-OZ1U. Accessed 11 Feb. 2021.
Pg. 79: "Influential Women in Stem." Influential Women in STEM Quotes. *The Networking and Information Technology Research and Development Program*. 31 March 2020: https://www.nitrd.gov/womens-history-month/influential-stem-quotes/. Accessed 11 Feb. 2021.
Pg. 81: "Quotes by Amelia Earhart." (n.d.). *Amelia Earhart*. https://www.ameliaearhart.com/quotes/. Accessed 11 Feb. 2021.
Pg. 83: "Influential Women in Stem." Influential Women in STEM Quotes. *The Networking and Information Technology Research and Development Program*. 31 March 2020: https://www.nitrd.gov/womens-history-month/influential-stem-quotes/. Accessed 11 Feb. 2021.
Pg. 85: Rizvi, Ahmed. "The Fall and Rise of Maturing Serena Williams." *Sport*, 10 Sept. 2021, https://www.thenationalnews.com/sport/the-fall-and-rise-of-maturing-serena-williams-1.632294. Accessed 11 Feb. 2021.
Pg. 87: McClung, Nellie. *Merna Forster, 100 Canadian Heroes*. 2004. Compiled by QuotationsByWomen.com, (n.d.), https://quotationsbywomen.com/. Accessed 11 Feb. 2021.
Pg. 89: "Ms. Foundation for Women on Indigenous Peoples' Day." *Ms. Foundation for Women*. 12 Oct. 2020: https://forwomen.org/indigenous-peoples-day-2020/. Accessed 11 Feb. 2021.
Pg. 91: "11 Messages of Female Empowerment From Women in Hollywood." *BuzzFeed*, 23 Feb. 2015, https://www.buzzfeed.com/jarettwieselman/11-empowering-messages-from-women-in-hollywood. Accessed 11 Feb. 2021.
Pg. 93: Dowd, Maureen. "Lady of the Rings: Jacinda Rules." *The New York Times*, 8 Sept. 2018, https://www.nytimes.com/2018/09/08/opinion/sunday/jacinda-ardern-new-zealand-prime-minister.html. Accessed 11 Feb. 2021.
Pg. 95: "Melinda French Gates – Powerful Voices Annual Luncheon." Press Room Speeches. *Bill & Melinda Gates Foundation*. 16 Oct. 2003: https://www.gatesfoundation.org/Media-Center/Speeches/2003/10/Melinda-French-Gates-2003-Powerful-Voices-Luncheon. Accessed 11 Feb. 2021.
Pg. 97: Harjo, Joy. "A Q&A with Joy Harjo, poet laureate of the United States." Interviewed by Elizabeth Lund. *The Christian Science Monitor*. 1 April 2020. https://www.csmonitor.com/Books/Author-Q-As/2020/0401/A-Q-A-with-Joy-Harjo-poet-laureate-of-the-United-States. Accessed 11 Feb. 2021.
Pg. 99: "Clara Barton A Lifetime Of Service." *Clara Barton National Historic Site*. National Park Service. (n.d.), https://www.nps.gov/clba/learn/historyculture/upload/cbservice.pdf. Accessed 11 Feb. 2021.
Pg. 101: "Four of Our Favorite Reese Witherspoon Quotes From Reese Witherspoon's May Cover Story." *InStyle*, 28 April 2015, https://www.instyle.com/news/four-our-favorite-quotes-witherspoons-may-cover-story. Accessed 11 Feb. 2021.
Pg. 103: "Joan Baez." *Oxford Essential Quotations*. Online. Oxford University Press, 2016, https://www.oxfordreference.com/view/10.1093/acref/9780191826719.001.0001/q-oro-ed4-00011975. Accessed 11 Feb. 2021.
Pg. 105: Keys, Alicia. "Alicia Keys Reflects On How Life Experiences Gave Her Permission To Be 'More Myself.'" Interviewed by Noel King. *NPR*, 27 March 2020, https://www.npr.org/2020/03/27/821654852/alicia-keys-reflects-on-how-life-experiences-gave-her-permission-to-be-more-myse. Accessed 11 Feb. 2021.
Pg. 107: Johnson, Katherine. "NASA Pioneer: Katherine Johnson Q&A." Interviewed by Sue Lindsey. *AARP*, 19 Feb. 2018, https://www.aarp.org/politics-society/history/info-2018/katherine-johnson-fd.html. Accessed 11 Feb. 2021.
Pg. 109: "11 Famous Women on Female Empowerment." *Saturday Night Live*, (n.d.). Compiled by *InStyle*, 17 Jan. 2017, https://www.instyle.com/celebrity/famous-women-female-empowerment?slide=2678c2de-ba87-49a5-bf5a-2186150ed2fe#2678c2de-ba87-49a5-bf5a-2186150ed2fe. Accessed 11 Feb. 2021.

Photo Attributions

Cover: Photo by Tonktiti, https://www.shutterstock.com/image-photo/copy-space-silhouette-woman-raise-hand-1490563400, royalty-free image, (image was manipulated)

Pg. 5-6: Photo by Biletskiy_Evgeniy, https://www.gettyimages.com/detail/photo/mountain-landscape-royalty-free-image/591441250, royalty-free image, (no changes were made)

Pg. 7: Malala Yousafzai, licensed under the CC Attribution-Share Alike 2.0 Generic license - https://creativecommons.org/licenses/by/2.0/legalcode, photo by Simon Davis/DFID (no changes were made)

Pg. 9: Maya Angelou, licensed under the CC Attribution-Share Alike 2.0 Generic license - https://creativecommons.org/licenses/by-sa/2.0/legalcode, photo by John Mathew Smith (image was lightened)

Pg. 11: Jane Goodall, licensed under CC Attribution-Share Alike 3.0 Unported license - https://creativecommons.org/licenses/by-sa/3.0/legalcode, photo by Floatjon (no changes were made)

Pg. 13: Susan B. Anthony, {{PD-US}} - a U.S. work that is in the public domain in the U.S. for an unspecified reason, but presumably because it was published in the U.S. before 1925.

Pg. 15: Kamala Harris, photo is a work is in the public domain in the United States

Pg. 17: Beyoncé, photo is a work is in the public domain in the United States

Pg. 19: Sonia Sotomayor, photo is a work is in the public domain in the United States

Pg. 21: Anne Lamott, licensed under CC Attribution-Share Alike 3.0 Unported license - https://creativecommons.org/licenses/by-sa/3.0/legalcode, photo by Zboralski (no changes were made)

Pg. 23: Michelle Obama, photo is a work is in the public domain in the United States

Pg. 25: Tawakkol Karman, licensed under the CC Attribution-Share Alike 4.0 International license - https://creativecommons.org/licenses/by-sa/4.0/legalcode, photo by Jindrich Nosek (no changes were made)

Pg. 27: Arundhati Roy, licensed under the CC Attribution-Share Alike 2.0 Generic license - https://creativecommons.org/licenses/by-sa/2.0/legalcode, photo by jeanbaptisteparis (no changes were made)

Pg. 29: Rita Moreno, licensed under the CC Attribution-Share Alike 2.0 Generic license - https://creativecommons.org/licenses/by-sa/2.0/legalcode, photo by John Mathew Smith (no changes were made)

Pg. 31: Laverne Cox, licensed under CC Attribution-Share Alike 3.0 Unported license - https://creativecommons.org/licenses/by-sa/3.0/legalcode, photo by Sachyn Mital (no changes were made)

Pg. 33: Maryam Mirzakhani, licensed under the CC Attribution-Share Alike 4.0 International license - https://creativecommons.org/licenses/by-sa/4.0/legalcode, photo by Amanda Phingbodhipakkiya (no changes were made)

Pg. 35: Elizabeth Gilbert, licensed under the CC Attribution-Share Alike 2.0 Generic license - https://creativecommons.org/licenses/by-sa/2.0/legalcode, photo by Erik Charlton (no changes were made)

Pg. 37: Mary Wollstonecraft, {{PD-US}} - a U.S. work that is in the public domain in the U.S. for an unspecified reason, but presumably because it was published in the U.S. before 1925.

Pg. 39: Leymah Gbowee, licensed under the CC Attribution-Share Alike 2.0 Generic license - https://creativecommons.org/licenses/by-sa/2.0/legalcode, photo by Fronteiras do Pensamento (no changes were made)

Pg. 41: Delores Huerta, licensed under the CC Attribution-Share Alike 2.0 Generic license - https://creativecommons.org/licenses/by-sa/2.0/legalcode, photo by John Mathew Smith & www.celebrity-photos.com (image was lightened)

Pg. 43: Winona LaDuke, licensed under the CC Attribution-Share Alike 2.0 Generic license - https://creativecommons.org/licenses/by-sa/2.0/legalcode, photo by Sarah Deer (image was sharpened)

Pg. 45: Marie Curie, {{PD-US}} - a U.S. work that is in the public domain in the U.S. for an unspecified reason, but presumably because it was published in the U.S. before 1925

Pg. 47: Maya Lin, licensed under the CC Attribution-Share Alike 2.0 Generic license - https://creativecommons.org/licenses/by-sa/2.0/legalcode, photo by Forgemind ArchiMedia (no changes were made)

Pg. 49: Ntozake Shange, licensed under CC Attribution-Share Alike 3.0 Unported license - https://creativecommons.org/licenses/by-sa/3.0/legalcode, photo by Barnard College (no changes were made)

Pg. 51: Amy Schumer, licensed under the CC Attribution-Share Alike 2.0 Generic license - https://creativecommons.org/licenses/by-sa/2.0/legalcode, photo by Greg2600 (no changes were made)

Pg. 53: Coretta Scott King, licensed under CC by 2.0 - https://creativecommons.org/licenses/by/2.0/legalcode, photo by Kingkongphoto & www.celebrity-photos.com (no changes were made)

Pg. 55: Audre Lorde, licensed under CC Attribution-Share Alike 3.0 Unported license - https://creativecommons.org/licenses/by-sa/3.0/legalcode, licensed under CC Attribution 2.5 Generic license - https://creativecommons.org/licenses/by/2.5/legalcode, photo by photo by Elsa Dorfman (photo was color corrected)
Pg. 57: Eleanor Roosevelt, photo is a work is in the public domain in the United States
Pg. 59: Corazon Aquino, photo is a work is in the public domain in the United States
Pg. 61: Diana Ross, photo is a work is in the public domain in the United States
Pg. 63: Marlene Dietrich, photo is a work is in the public domain in the United States
Pg. 65: Shirley Chisholm, photo is a work is from the U.S. News & World Report collection at the Library of Congress
Pg. 67: Yoko Ono, licensed under the CC Attribution-Share Alike 2.0 Generic license - https://creativecommons.org/licenses/by/2.0/legalcode, photo by The Peabody Awards (no changes were made)
Pg. 69: Alice Walker, licensed under the CC Attribution-Share Alike 2.0 Generic license - https://creativecommons.org/licenses/by/2.0/legalcode, photo by Virginia DeBolt (no changes were made)
Pg. 71: Meg Whitman, licensed under the CC Attribution-Share Alike 2.0 Generic license - https://creativecommons.org/licenses/by/2.0/legalcode, photo by Max Morse (photo was lightened)
Pg. 73: Frida Kahlo, {{PD-US}} - a U.S. work that is in the public domain in the U.S. for an unspecified reason, but presumably because it was published in the U.S. before 1925
Pg. 75: Elizabeth Blackwell, {{PD-US}} - a U.S. work that is in the public domain in the U.S. for an unspecified reason, but presumably because it was published in the U.S. before 1925
Pg. 77: Ruth Bader Ginsburg, photo is a work of a United States federal court judge or magistrate judge, taken or made as part of that person's official duties
Pg. 79: Mae Jemison, photo is in the public domain in the United States because it was solely created by NASA
Pg. 81: Amelia Earhart, photo is a work is in the public domain in the United States
Pg. 83: Lise Meitner, image was taken from Flickr's The Commons: no known copyright restrictions
Pg. 85: Serena Williams, licensed under the CC Attribution-Share Alike 2.0 Generic license - https://creativecommons.org/licenses/by/2.0/legalcode, photo by Edwin Martinez (no changes were made)
Pg. 87: Nellie McClung, this Canadian work is in the public domain in Canada because its copyright has expired, also a U.S. work that is in the public domain in the U.S. for an unspecified reason, but presumably because it was published in the U.S. before 1925
Pg. 89: Wilma Mankiller, licensed under CC Attribution-Share Alike 3.0 Unported license - https://creativecommons.org/licenses/by-sa/3.0/legalcode, photo by Philkon Phil Konstantin (no changes were made)
Pg. 91: Viola Davis, licensed under the CC Attribution-Share Alike 2.0 Generic license - https://creativecommons.org/licenses/by/2.0/legalcode, photo by RedCarpetReport (no changes were made)
Pg. 93: Jacinda Ardern, licensed under the Creative Commons Attribution-Share Alike 3.0 New Zealand - https://creativecommons.org/licenses/by-sa/3.0/nz/legalcode, photo by Labour Party (no changes were made)
Pg. 95: Melinda Gates, licensed under CC Attribution-Share Alike 3.0 Unported license - https://creativecommons.org/licenses/by-sa/3.0/legalcode, photo by Kjetil Ree (no changes were made)
Pg. 97: Joy Harjo, CC0 1.0 Universal Public Domain Dedication
Pg. 99: Clara Barton, photo is a work is in the public domain in the United States
Pg. 101: Reese Witherspoon, licensed under the CC Attribution-Share Alike 2.0 Generic license - https://creativecommons.org/licenses/by/2.0/legalcode, photo by dtstuff9 (no changes were made)
Pg. 103: Joan Baez, work was obtained from the now defunct United States Information Agency
Pg. 105: Alicia Keys, licensed under the CC Attribution-Share Alike 2.0 Generic license - https://creativecommons.org/licenses/by/2.0/legalcode, photo by Eva Rinaldi (photo was lightened and sharpened)
Pg. 107: Katherine Johnson, photo is in the public domain in the United States because it was solely created by NASA
Pg. 109: Tina Fey, licensed under the CC Attribution-Share Alike 2.0 Generic license - https://creativecommons.org/licenses/by/2.0/legalcode, photo by Mingle Media TV (no changes were made)
Pg. 111-112: Photo by Marekuliasz, https://www.gettyimages.com/detail/photo/winter-canoe-paddling-in-colorado-royalty-free-image/507676184, royalty-free image, (image was reversed)
Pg. 113-114: Photo by Sasint, https://pixabay.com/photos/cliff-adventure-above-hiking-1822484/, royalty-free image, (no changes were made)

www.ingramcontent.com/pod-product-compliance
Lightning Source LLC
Chambersburg PA
CBHW061210070526
44583CB00025B/3186